FEAR OF MOVING WATER

Fear of Moving Water

Alex Grant

WIND PUBLICATIONS

International Standard Book Number 978-1-936138-02-9
Library of Congress Control Number 2009934648

First edition

Cover photograph — "Evening Wake" by Dan Albergotti

ACKNOWLEDGMENTS

I offer thanks to the editors of the following publications and contests, where these poems first appeared or were acknowledged.

Chains & Mirrors, North Carolina Writers' Network (Harperprints, 2006) — Twenty-one of these poems made up this 2006 Randall Jarrell Poetry Prize-winning chapbook.

The Oscar Arnold Young Award — *Chains & Mirrors* received this award in 2007 (Best North Carolina poetry collection in the previous year.)

The White Book (Main St. Rag Publishing, 2008) — Twenty-two of these poems made up this chapbook.

Cream City Review — "Authenticity of the Bones" (Re-printed *Poetry Southeast*)

Sycamore Review — "Interpreting the Silence"

Arts & Letters — "Secret Sonnet for the Cockroach" (Honorable mention, 2004 Poetry Prize, nominated for *Best New Poets 2005* anthology); "A History of Foot-Beating" (Honorable mention, 2005 Poetry Prize, nominated for *Best New Poets 2006* anthology); "Fuel," "His Holiness the Abbot," "Sugar," "Lenticular" and "Frequent Existentialist" were finalists for the 2006 *Arts & Letters* Rumi Poetry Prize.

Midwest Quarterly — "Black Moon" (First printed Winter 2005, also selected to appear in 50th-anniversary commemorative issue, Summer 2009); "How the Cuckoo Sings" (Finalist, NCSU 2005 contest)

Poet Lore — "Hostilities In Bangalore"

Sow's Ear Poetry Review — "The Steps of Montmartre" (Finalist, 2004 Poetry Contest.)

Phi Kappa Phi Forum — "Poetry Final"

Cimarron Review — "Sonnet on the Lines on Your Hand," "Preserved in Amber"

Connecticut Review — "Captain Scott's Lost Diary"

Rhapsoidia — "Continental Divides"

Seattle Review — "Giant" (2006 *Best New Poets* anthology alternate.)

Nimrod — "Dreaming in Gethsemane," "Neruda's Suicide Note," "Valediction," "Thread" (Honorable mentions, 2005 Pablo Neruda

Prize. "Gethsemane" re-printed *Poetry Southeast*); "Hamish Samey's Turnip Soup," "The Curse of Tourette"

The Pavel Srut Fellowship in Poetry — "The Curse of Tourette," "Poetry Final," "Vespers," "The Steps of Montmartre," "Black Moon" and "Dreaming in Gethsemane" were among a group of ten poems which received this award in 2004.

Best New Poets 2007— "The Steps of Montmartre" (nominated by *Poemeleon*).

Sunken Garden Poetry Chapbook Contest — Twenty of these poems made up the chapbook *Fear of Moving Water*, one of six 2006 contest finalists.

"Discovery" / The Nation — "Black Moon," "Neruda's Suicide Note," "The Steps of Montmartre," "His Holiness The Abbot," "Vespers," "Secret Sonnet for The Cockroach," "Madonna & Child," "Lenticular," "A History of Foot-Beating," "How The Cuckoo Sings" and "Authenticity of The Bones" were 2005 finalists & 2006 alternates for the award.

Kakalak Carolina Poets Anthology 2006 — "Argentina's Huge Beaver Problem" (First Prize, 2006 contest)

Kakalak Carolina Poets Anthology 2007 (Special guest contributor) — "Sugar," "Transubstantiation," "Poetry Mid-term," "There's Love and Death and in Between You Eat and Drink"

Kakalak Carolina Poets Anthology 2008 — "Palimpsest" (Honorable mention, 2008 contest)

Eleventh Muse — "Resurrection"

Poemeleon — "Sonnet For The Educated Cook," "The Steps of Montmartre" (reprint), "There's Love and Death and in Between You Eat and Drink" (reprint)

Main St. Rag — "Night Sequence," "Frequent Existentialist," "Angiogram"

Thanks for indulgence and encouragement, both personal and poetic, to Tristi DeBlander, Roy Jacobstein, Margaret Rabb and Tom Lisk. Thanks also to Robert Penn Warren for his posthumous thunderbolt.

Contents

3 – *Cocked & Benedictive*

4 – *Chains & Mirrors*

For Tristi

1

Bones & Confetti

So we come here, to this haberdashery of words, apothecary for the faintly damaged. Well, Wounded Elk, walk this way – follow the voice leading you toward something, anything other than that damned catechism of caterwauling you've suffered through the shrinking years of bones and confetti – The lights will go down and the yellow spotlight of the moon will pull your body upward from the slow riptide of the world.

BLACK MOON

I watch him drag the boat across
　the scree, over the dry doggerel
　　of mackerel scales and filament

of a season ended, to the water.
　The sand flays the last flakes
　　of paint from the boat's hull,

splash and crack at the confluence
　of stone and water, and he is out
　　beyond the waves, where fishbones

glint like small suns in a black mirror,
　and the splay of the Pelican's wing
　　stitches the sea to the sky. Brine-

bleached hands haul the sodden creel
　above the gunwales, and there again
　　is the gaping child-shaped hole,

sawn by the snapping turtle's teeth,
　ragged-cut and impossible to mend.
　　Did I say that the turtle is guided

by ambient moonlight? So, the wolf
　howls. The waves gnaw at the shore.
　　Bones and light are mixed with water.

ARGENTINA'S HUGE BEAVER PROBLEM

Giant Beavers Flood Land of Fire
— Reuter's

Whether this title relates to outsized rodents
or some enormous beaveresque conundrum

withers if you know that in Tierra Del Fuego
they pay a dollar a tail, a gnawing diminution

of this "large aquatic rodent of the genus *Castor*"
(fathered by Zeus in the form of a swan – born

from an egg with Pollux, his twin – protectors
of sailors, whose brotherly love flickers nightly

in the constellation Gemini, under whose white
stars gauchos tote their *boleadoras*, beef hooves

waiting for entanglement – spindly fore-legs
propping up mounds of meat in this bloody

menagerie – etymology old French *ménage* –
add in *à trois* and we're back to the beaver.)

At The End of the World, the Pampas
are flooding – the Paranà river gushing

over cut-banks of Lenga and Guindo –
oceans pouring into oceans, flat-land

inundation in the mouth of black water,
ground down by the smallest white teeth.

AUTHENTICITY OF THE BONES

"When you were young, you walked
where you would, but when you are old,
you will stretch out your hands, and another
will carry you where you do not wish to go."
　　　　　— Jesus' prophecy to St. Peter

The bones of St. Peter,
mortified Saint,
unearthed, almost complete,
except for his feet, shattered
in the act of crucifixion –
and the mouse bones
found by his skeleton –
the only certainties being
that one is a mouse
and one is a man.

Guided by our voices,
the lacuna of years leaves
us holding only fragments –
like these brittle shards
of language they left behind –
"aedicula, liturgy, sacrament" –
chants of the rope-dancers
writhing through Necropolis –
preserved, like the perfect bones
of the mouse, and the fable
of the man, and the Saint
dancing still without his feet.

7

THE STEPS OF MONTMARTRE

— after Brassai's 1936 photograph

On the steps of Sacre Coeur
  Cathedral, in that same winter
    when *junge leute* filled Bavarian

beer-gardens, ten years before
  Adorno proclaimed that there
    could be no art after Auschwitz,

Brassai captured his flawless
  image. Through the tunnel
    formed by the parting trees,

battalions of lamp-posts advance
  and retreat in the morning mizzle,
    clamp chain-link handrails hard

into sunwashed cobbles. In less
  than a year, the corpseless heads
    on Nanking's walls will coalesce

with Guernica's ruined heart, *mal
  du siècle* will become *Weltschmerz,*
    and the irresistible symmetry

of a million clacking bootheels
  will deafen half a continent.
    The red brush never dries –

adagio leads finally to fugue,
  haiku to satori, and the image
    fixed in silver to remembering.

NERUDA'S SUICIDE NOTE

— In memory of Spalding Gray

They say nothing ever changes
but your point of view.
Nothing – "*some thing*
that has no existence" –
this makes no sense.
I sit in the catacumbas
and listen to the rain
pound the papaya leaves –
my skin like confetti,
my heart a cheap lottery.

I have seen the tiger's stripes –
they live between
the fine linen sheets
of an office-girl's bed,
in the afternoon fumblings
of someone who is no-one,
with a heart bursting
like a red balloon
on a tap – the pieces fly
in all directions, you cover
your face with your hand,
and it sticks to your skin
like confetti, like phosphorus
launched from a Greek warship,
like the skin of a plum
peeled by a broken nail.

SECRET SONNET FOR THE COCKROACH

They live without their bodies for a week,
you know – subsisting on the head, the mind
alone – they flit like frogs beside a creek
whenever pounding footsteps come to grind
their crunchy shells into some pristine hard-
wood floor. You stamp on one, and six white eggs
are jettisoned inside a fibrous shard
they say is tougher than a whiskey keg.
Four billion years and evolution's passed
them by – this crevice-living dinosaur,
resisting every futile fog and gas-
filled labyrinth – unlike the Minotaur –
bull-headed, eggless doorman of the maze –
that mythic locus Theseus embraced.

GIANT

I read once that garden midges only live for around
ten minutes, and as I watched a swarm of them, I picked
one out, kept my eyes fixed on him, lit a cigarette, and tried
to imagine his life. I did the math, and decided that eight
midge seconds equaled one of our years, and as he moved
from the top to the bottom of the cloud, he had two affairs
and a nervous breakdown right there. He spiraled up again,
and by the time he'd reached the top, he'd sent all seventeen-
hundred of his children to a fashionable private swarm in the
upper reaches of a more desirable neighboring tree. He'd
gained a little weight by now, and couldn't fly quite as fast
as he used to, but he compensated by quietly negotiating
his own private air-space, and by employing some of the
younger midges to bite people for him. By the time my
cigarette had burned less than half-way down, he'd written
a number of wildly successful self-help flying manuals,
as well as his acclaimed study of midge relationships –
'Female midges are from the eastern boughs, male midges
are from the western.' He'd had liposuction and wing implants
by this time, and was campaigning tirelessly to have the trashy
cloud in the next tree publicly censured. His therapist advised
him to adopt a lower public profile, but he was insistent that
he alone had secured the swarm's tenure of the tree, and that
the other midges ought to damn-well recognize his contribution
and reward him accordingly. He died three quarters of the way
into my cigarette, convinced that the rest of the swarm
were plotting to run him down with a golf-cart.

He was truly a giant among midges.

THE CURSE OF TOURETTE

"Enfer foutu!"
  — Gilles de la Tourette

In Arles, Domaine de la Tourette,
  Gauguin painted 'Self-portrait
    dedicated to Vincent Van Gogh,'

who held a straight razor
  to his throat, then reeking
    of absinthe and remorse,

sliced off his ear because he
  "didn't need to hear the paint."
    Ten years later, in the asylum

at Lausanne, Gilles de la Tourette,
  the man cursed by the affliction
    named for him, died in obscurity.

They met, briefly, in eighteen
  eighty-four, *Meneer* Van Gogh
    and *Monsieur* de la Tourette, each

touched by the flickering light
  of near-recognition, each naive
    to the impending flux – each

oblivious to the connections
  being forged and the black
    crows circling overhead.

LILLIAN GISH'S MIRROR

Silk curtains swish
quiet as a stage-whisper,
signal an encore performance
at the academy of flesh.
Around this silvered screen,
the once-red bulbs, now
chiffon-pink, hum
their faint applause.
A quiet acceptance,
beatitude of years, pervades
her shrinking days
and every day
the mirror darkens,
the Buddha's face moves closer,
one golden eye opening
like a spreading Lotus blossom
floating on a black pool.

HOSTILITIES IN BANGALORE

The Chai-wallah squats, cracks his nicotine grin,
and begins the morning ritual. He pours
the steaming tea backward and forward

between the brass brewing pots, steady and sure
in his movement, an artist in water and metal
and leaves, a shaman showman of the everyday.

His tea-boys look on, each dreaming of the day
when the boy becomes the master, when the world
will burst open like a fat flower. For now,

they hold tight the small bowls he hands
to each of them, waiting for his guru tap
on their foreheads, the admonishing wave

of his finger. All around them, battalions
of young girls with bare arms, skin the color
of melted butter, troop past to catch the early

train, disappear into the locomotive hiss
like soft dough falling in hot oil. The tea-boys
spatter out from the Chai-wallah's feet, each

rushing for a window, tea-bowls held aloft
like sacramental offerings, moving, in these brief
moments of truce, one day closer to some imagined

independence. From the end of the marshal-yard,
the station master squints at the clock, ticking down
the customary two minutes of commerce, this small

armistice on his watch, then moves to swat
the tea-boys from the windows. He marches
to the end of the platform, then spins around

and whistles, and his oblivious army advances again
on the city. As the train retreats from the station,
the little general lights a bidi and struts the platform,

waiting for the next train, waiting for the end
of some familiar, yet un-nameable hostility.

2

Bodies & Water

They were fishing the bodies out for days – bloated curds of humanity. The salt had turned most of them white. Random immensity of the world. Scientists claim there's a universe closer to your skin than the clothes you wear – this may explain why you feel like someone else is in the room. And time never was a straight line – it bends like a piece of elbow spaghetti – the big noodle, cosmic boomerang, good old time.

IN THE OCEAN, BONES FLASH
LIKE WHITE STARS IN WINTER

— Solo renga, after Basho

White pelicans swoop
Over black breaking wave-caps –
Yellow moon rising.

No stars in the sky
you can see – they're there, of course,
Behind yellow clouds,

Small pinholes of hope,
Catechisms of permanence
In the shifting void.

The wise man knows that
The sea, the gull, the salmon
All contain the world.

The ocean tells us
The future is a black wave
Twelve stories high – how

The dog-dreams of home
Sustain the spirit in its
Winter battlefield!

A man has five thoughts –
Boiled-down bones, childhood, dreams, blood.
Continuation.

INTERPRETING THE SILENCE

'Behind every jewel stand three hundred sweating horses'
— Zen Buddhist aphorism

Believers in invisibility, we describe the sound
that nothing makes. At night, we hear the stars
move across the sky, listen to the moon-vine

grow, wait for the engines of the sun to crack
the morning. The clacking wheels of desire
lead us to this – this endless fascination, this

capturing of fog in a bottle. We need to inhale
it, to learn its given name, to feel it compress
under the skin and emerge through the pores,

an invisible diamond inside a painted nutshell,
held tight in the breath of our hands. We pry
the shell apart, clamp the empty geodes to our

ears, like seashore children straining to hear
the wedding of the oceans in a paper cup,
and listen to the sound that nothing makes.

VESPERS

for V.

Five-thirty and the crickets
    are already out – November
        twilight crowds in through

the winnowed elms. My old
    Chow's claws click on slick
        hardwood, signal the growling

appetite, constant as her yelp,
    undiminished by the years
        of splintered tooth and bone.

She guzzles at the water-bowl,
    each unlikely lick spattering
        the bleached skirting boards.

Outside, night is filling the sky.
    The generator's mosquito-hum
        briefly quietens a red birdsong.

I look up the meaning of *vespers*,
    find "Four psalms, a capitulum,
        a response, a hymn, a versicle,

a canticle from the Gospel, litany
    (*Kyrie eleison, Christe eleison*), Pater
        with the ordinary finale, *oratio*,

or prayer, and dismissal." She
    will go south soon, escape
        the confines of this fading

daylight, to another latitude,
    on a chart known only to her,
        red, quiet and roofless.

THE LONG, SLOW DROP

A wedge of salted cantaloupe
sinking in blue agave.

A bruised peach
in a white porcelain bowl.

The heart's iambic thud,
like steps on maple floors.

Four strands of hair
in a lover's mouth.

A zinc nail sunk in bitumen.

A black-haired boy
seen in a rear-view mirror.

A plum tomato skewered
on a bamboo stave.

A Chinese flag buckled
in the monsoon's lull.

The white afternoon
turning to November dark.

HIS HOLINESS THE ABBOT
IS SHITTING IN THE WITHERED FIELDS

— after Buson

The mortal frame, the Haiku Masters hold,
is made up of one hundred bones
and nine orifices.

The mind this frame contains can be used,
or not used, to make the poem,
or become the poem.

Becoming is accomplished without thought,
making requires the application
of intent and will.

All change comes from objects in motion.
To capture the thing at rest, you
must be moving.

So, 7 days bereaved, Issa made his father's
death poem: *"A bath when you're born,
a bath when you die – how stupid."*

Grief is a silk neckerchief covering a burn
around the throat, holding sound
down in the body.

And so we make these sounds without
thought – the heretic body burns,
intends, and moves.

HOW THE CUCKOO SINGS

How like the cuckoo,
singing on the mountain-top –
Spring's last moon setting.

After singing eight thousand and eight
songs, the mountain cuckoo, the Haiku
Masters said, vomits blood and dies.

Then, all things contained life: the stone,
the cup, the pitchfork – *the scent of life* –
carried on the spinning of every atom.

The bridge spanning the worlds of *satori*
and the everyday was made visible to men
by "the selfless, diligent practice of *Haiku.*"

The body knows before the mind, feels
enlightenment's temporary flash,
approaching Kundalini's electric arc.

The sake cup and the overturned bowl,
swept away in the morning dust, hold
nothing less and more than life itself –

eight thousand and eight songs.

SUGAR

— *For the Haiku Master Issa, and his father*

19 days into the late spring moon,
Issa pours sugar down his father's
throat, rubs his feet and shoulders,

listens, in the early hours, to breath
labor like fading wind. He watches
him mouth unheard prayers, hears

the rattle in the gullet, the invitation
to the moon to walk with him again.
Delirium comes in many forms, but

none so blatant as necessity, none
so welcome as the inevitable stone
sinking back into amniotic blue.

FUEL

We spend the morning burning
oleander brush. Shards of sunlight
slash the canopy, cleave pathways

through pungent smoke-shrouds,
fuel clumps of emerald sphagnum.
By late afternoon, wilted leaves unfurl

over smoldering white boneyards
of sap and lignite – we forage through
small charred universes, hunting for stars.

We slough off the day's skins,
pull on clean shirts, watch waning
light wash over the high loblolly tops –

Vesper sits low on the eastern
horizon, semaphoric Pleiades winks
through the flapping sycamore leaves –

nightfall's slow swirl beckons.
I raise a glass to Atlas, see Orion's
belt of pearls through swirling amber,

then think of Li Po, drowned
trying to grab the moon's reflection
in the river, undone by the innocent sin

of possession, one drunken act's
inexorable gravity dragging the body
down to the place where stars extinguish.

LENTICULAR

The pier is half-gone, black pylons jutting
  fifty yards from shore, the bait and tackle
    shop turned into a Tiki Pub. A blonde waif

tends bar, ministering to the unholy needs
  of the old salt perched on the peeling stool.
    He squints sideways in my direction, lists

to starboard and blows a pale blue cloud
  in Blondie's face. I take my pink polystyrene
    pakeke and the bakelite ashtray she scudded

down the bar-top and walk the planks
  to the far Eastern rail – Pacific rip tides
    pummel stanchions sunk when Bismarck

was still swaying in his governess's arms. So
  much unseen activity under the opaque waves –
    like shoals of trigger-fish scuttling to fertilize

flotillas of bobbing eggs – frenzied clouding
  explained away by the calm biology of ganglion
    and axion, the clustered nerve and inexplicable

attraction named, as if by naming we could
  pin the unknowable, the way we name clouds –
    Cirrus, Fractostratus, Cumulonimbus, Mammatus.

RESURRECTION

Death is not the worst evil.
                    — Sophocles

Lazarus, raised from mediocrity,
moves to a small desert town.
Mornings, he chases
his *kibbutznik* anonymity
behind the goat-herd's
clattering hooves, watches
the Juniper leaves tear
the sky like green stigmata,
holds the white pistils
of un-named flowers
in his pristine hands –
cupped and cuneiform,
capable of holding universes.
Nights, he takes the moon
down through the trees, bends
his fingers around its halo,
presses his thumbs
into its tearless crater eyes –
"suffer, you bastard"
he thinks – "suffer."

NIGHT SEQUENCE

Moonrise

> Dog-stars muzzled
> by the hunchback moon –
> the machinery of night.

Shadow

> In another country,
> men forge guillotines
> from discarded spoons.

Oblivion

> The operations of night
> will feed your shrinking skin
> to the desert of years.

Celestial Mechanics

> In heaven, the machines
> will be dismantled
> one breath at a time.

Gods

> God of verbs and nouns,
> moving heaven and earth
> closer to your eyes.

3

Cocked & Benedictive

Two days wrangling with the beast and I flip it on its back. I slap my hands in triumph and the world agrees with me – the air-conditioner hums into life between the first and second claps. Sunday twilight – A farmer's John Deere clanks and clatters its metallic symphony a mile across the meadow. Vincent's spirit paints a bleeding sunset – I know he's crazy, but humor him anyway….

DREAMING IN GETHSEMANE

Then one of the criminals who were hanged
blasphemed Him, saying, "If You are the Christ,
save Yourself and us."
          — Luke 23:39

He dreams of undiscovered Cuba or El Salvador,
their seductive anonymity and promise
of disease. He will evaporate slowly there,
one breath at a time, and watch the paint of his life
dry on some colonial wall. He will hang
suspended from a rope swing, wearing his empty
hat, and watch thin fingers of cloud drop
a red ball into a noiseless ocean. He will feed
the starving appetites of youth again, taste the moon
on his tongue, feel the stars swell in his belly.

In the local *baro*, swarming with late-afternoon
barflies and sunlit dust, the men who huddle
in corners will invent the colors of his past,
and talk in whispers of this dark-skinned *gringo*
who has caused Don Sibrento's widow to eat guava
again. Together, they will rewrite the history of love
on a grain of sand, and talk of their lives in future
tenses. His heart will swell again, bigger than any saint's,
and when he passes, the people of the village
will throw black roses from the graveside.

They will compose songs of youth in his honor,
and name a feast-day for him, and in time
his memory will fade and mingle with the dust
that blows into the eyes of children and cattle,
and no-one but Dona Sibrento will recall his name.

POETRY MID-TERM

[1]

Describe the smell when rain hits the pavement
after a long dry spell. Discuss the importance
of the following factors: the rain, the nose,
the builder of the road, propensity for language.

[2]

Imagine that the universe is small enough
to fit between the covers of a book.
Invent a character who convinces everyone
of the boundless nature of the cosmos.
You may not use the omniscient form.

[3]

Explain the color blue (all shades).
In less than three hundred words, propose
a new way of looking at a raindrop.
Cite a minimum of three practical applications.

[4]

Establish a credible connection between
the following: the curve of a woman's breast,
a 1957 Cadillac Imperial, monotheism. Result
must be enjoyable to the average reader,
and be small enough to hold in one hand.

[5]

True or False? You must change your life.

Sonnet for the Educated Cook

"A man who never cooks just isn't worth
a fuck," my grandad always said, while spuds
were boiling hard above the reeking hearth.
He'd plunge his wrinkled arms into the suds
and mutter something choice about the lack
of moral fibre in the world today,
how he could show those earring-wearing slack-
arsed bums that cooking is the only way
a man who cannot paint or write or dredge
a sound from any instrument can strive
to be the equal of the privileged,
those educated fools whose pointless lives
remind us of the need for making good
on promises to live the way we should.

CAPTAIN SCOTT'S LOST DIARY

"I'm just going outside, and may be some time"
                    — Captain Oates

Six weeks in this tent, and we are all close
to breaking-point. Captain Oates masturbates
constantly – even during dinner – he claims
it's simply a mechanism to keep his body temperature
up – though we all have our doubts. I no longer feel
comfortable shaking hands with him, and last night
he told me that he wants me to have his babies.
He insists on calling me "Falcon", though he knows
I detest my middle name. The natural order of things
seems to be breaking down – the men have begun
to question his authority of late, especially since
the unfortunate frozen-yogurt incident. My dear
wife is constantly in my thoughts – though Captain
Oates has taken to wearing a wig he made from
a penguin-skin, and insisting, in a ridiculous
falsetto impersonation of Mary, that I take him
to dinner at Claridge's. This strikes me as conduct
unbecoming of an English hero, but I find myself
strangely attracted by his buffoonish attempts at
humor, and on two occasions, have had to physically
restrain myself from mentioning his efforts
in dispatches. The wind is unrelenting, the cold
bites at every nerve, and Oates has threatened
that if we don't go to dinner soon, he'll go alone –
and that he may be gone for quite some time.

HAMISH SAMEY'S TURNIP SOUP

My Grandfather's neck would bulge
with veins thick as a horse's cock
when he swung the axe to the wood,
the thunk of metal on rings
cracking the morning air.
Wood flung on the fire,
flames swept upward
in the huge fart of the leather bellows,
screaming sparks crackling
up the black chimney.

Dark days, indeed, made bearable
only by the thick turnip soup
my Grandmother cauldron-boiled
over the wet peat heaved
from sullen bogs. Fat shards of pepper
would float like frog-spawn
in the turgid brew, daring
the faint-hearted to slurp down
the lung-sticking potage.
No stranger to daring myself,
I gobbled the turnip innards
like a starving goat in a midden.

O, red and purple-veined vegetable,
I stand before you now,
in this suburban supermarket,
consider your heft and proportions,
shiny, bulbous and stippled, waxy,
like my Grandmother's skin, purple
as my Grandfather's nose.

VALEDICTION

Mr. Stephens was old-school,
stalked the halls like a banshee,
his gown flying behind, launching
well-aimed pieces of chalk
at the heads of errant 12-year old boys.
Between periods of *Valerius At The Forum*
and *Sextus At The Circus Maximus,*
always quick to remind us,
on hearing of some ludicrous
soccer transfer fee, that the market value
of the human body was precisely
seven and fourpence-ha'penny,
and that there was no
such word as *pedibum.*
"My dad says it's a dead language,"
someone offered, an instant
before the chalk caromed
from the side of his head.
"Dog in a manger, boy –
dog in a manger."

"Elegy", you said, "is a mournful song,"
– like this irregular conjugation
of fumbling youth and age,
dogs and mangers,
and the chalk-white fingers
of the dead.

THERE'S LOVE AND DEATH
AND IN BETWEEN YOU EAT AND DRINK

There's Love and Death, and in between, you eat and drink.
The sun, the moon, the ocean's noiseless halls –
It really doesn't matter what you think.

Amphibious till the moment when you blink
Below the amniotic rain that squalls –
There's Love and Death, and in between, you eat and drink.

You burn new maps into the earth and link
The chains of memory where the daisy falls –
It really doesn't matter when you think.

You tie your knots and pay your dues in pink
And blues and green – even the hangman falls –
There's Love and Death, and in between, you eat and drink.

You hold your life up to your ear, you blink
And pound your head against the wailing walls –
It really doesn't matter how you think.

A thousand years from now, should these words chink
Your bones, this song will echo in your halls –
There's Love and Death, and in between, you eat and drink –
It really doesn't matter what you think.

MADONNA & CHILD

Ekphrasis after a photograph
of a Venezuelan flood victim

El Presidente clasps her shoulder,
thumb pressed profanely
into the hollow of her perfect
clavicle. Her dress, Caravaggio-red,
spaghetti-strapped, is pulled down
under one flawless breast,
above which his left hand hovers,
cocked and benedictive.
Under the ardent stares
of the usual cast of characters,
the nursing infant succors,
one fist raised in defiance,
rock versus scissors
in a flood of hands and nails,
naked skin and deliverance.

4

Chains & Mirrors

Here is the dirt road the color of honey, shocked by sundown's fading afterlight – past the boarded-up gas stations, the pock-marked asphalt, black and brittle as the waning moon – a million miles of beaten track end in a single step – the black boat floats on centuries of clear water.

A HISTORY OF FOOT-BEATING

Let he who does not know
what war is, go to war.
— Chinese proverb

In wine-bar diction, *bastinadoing* –
a beating with a cudgel or a stick –
is most effective when the giver sings
a marching song and squeezes on the prick
or balls or (God forbid) the nipples, while
the feet are being pummeled into black
and orange diabetic weals. This style
of quiet persuasion is now coming back
in favor with the thumbscrew set, who hate
to miss a chance to make a grown man piss,
while dreaming of the winding interstate
and contemplating those degrees of bliss
they find between the ball-peen's hollow crack
and *Kundalini* rising in the back.

Frequent Existentialist

Wheels down in New Hampshire (state motto:
"Exact change saves time.") Had a snorter
and a sniffer sitting kitty-corner, side by side,

(she, mid-life Malaysian mama – he, Generation
Y network support dude.) Suspect number three,
to my immediate right, is reading "Communion

with The Lord" and appears to have renounced
the arch-demon of deodorant and all his diabolic
works. I settle my head on the fuselage skin, flash

on fifties factories stamping out pink plastic
lampshades under banks of fluorescent lights.
I'm beginning to feel like Jean-Paul Sartre

with a hangover – and you, Simone, a thousand
miles away in a Carolina kitchen, pour egg-yolks
on a blue plate, small suns spattering china sky.

PRESERVED IN AMBER

One minute he's clipping the hair
from his ears, the next he's riding
that little wooden boat across some
nameless river. His wife walks
into the bathroom just as he flops
like a slab-fish whose spine has been cut
with one swift flick of the fillet-knife,
and she's screaming something about
JesusMaryMotherofGod, but he is somewhere
else now – careening through green fronds
in some half-recalled childhood pasture,
arms flailing like fleshy helicopter-blades,
whacking the heads of the red-hot pokers,
while the hot wax he carefully poured
into his fast-fading hair drips the length
of his face and clarifies on contact
with his quickly-cooling skin, like pine-sap
setting around the thin-veined wings
of some primordial moth, and his mouth
is forming the familiar frozen 'O', and someone
else will turn the pages of the trivial encyclopediae
of moth-wings and amber and helicopters, forgetful
of the pastures and the pokers and the fronds
waving like green banners in an endless parade.

FIRST LIGHT

The small mysteries remain,
    and the day has returned.

The phrase *in living memory* bubbles up
    Like a spring,
But I push it down and watch clouds
    Dark as burned paper
Scud across the white September sky.

Firepit sparks fly like lightning bugs,
    Brief and brilliant
In their tiny incarnations – universes of light

In the shrinking shadows –
Each universe defined by each observer –
    Creation and destruction
Transitory hand-maidens of autumn.

In the kingdom of smoke and mirrors, possibilities stretch
like train-tracks into the distance
    and the taste of mystery
never leaves the mouth.

THREAD

In the beginning, they were insignificant – like black
spider mites, or immature fruit flies. We were blind
to their subtle swelling, their shifting shapes

and colors, suddenly lurid green, slick and shiny
as obscene bottles. The years turned like a mill wheel,
and we retreated deeper into the belly of the house,

and few could recall a time when the steady hum
of their wings didn't thicken the air. One of us will
sometimes foray into their part of the house – always,

the reports are worse than the time before – they have
become cannibals: they devise new methods of torture:
their young subsist on the bodies of spiders.

And they grow – always – stronger, more ruthless.
We have lived so long in this part of the house,
where no light penetrates, that our young have begun

to be born blind – sightless, parchment skin stretched
over useless orbs, like unfinished paintings. Some
who remember when we lived outside of the house,

in the trees, in the fields and hedgerows, say that
our time will come again. They say that one day,
we will look up at the moon again, from high

in the wet branches of Sycamore trees,
and see the earth, so far below, and swing,
once again, on lengths of radiant silk.

Transubstantiation

— After Dali's *Metamorphosis of Narcissus*

A woman dreams she is an egg,
dripping through a stippled sky.

Aware now of nothing, mirror
for composition and color, her

chicken-hearted yellow yolk's
subtractive primaries, chalaza

and ovule connecting through
this stringy sheen of albumen,

the laminal nimbus, the haloed
husk of shell where movement

and sound take on importance –
the rhythm below the fontanelle

beats its metronomic imprint
like a coppersmith's hammer

melding unwhetted appetites
with the sharp clang of metal.

SONNET FOR THE TERRACOTTA WARRIORS

The adolescent Emperor Qinshihuang,
child ruler of the state of Qin, whose tomb
would one day hold three thousand wives, who rang
his bells with childless concubines in rooms
they flooded out with phosphorus when the act
was done, whose hollow-bodied warriors
and clay-foot horses melded with the black-
streaked mud of Xanxing's vanished borders –
whose sixty thousand laborers interred
beside his mummified remains might make
you think of egomania (preferred
affliction of the despot) – built a lake
of mercury to catch the rising sun,
and couldn't count beyond the number one.

PALIMPSEST

The currency of language is miniscule,
Cragged, unforgiving –
       Like the minutiae of coastlines.
Even grains of sand have space between.

What binds language is what clumps the earth –
Belief, it seems – belief in the word, in the scabrous fingertip –
Vessels containing vessels containing nothing
But themselves, *matryoshka* of tongue and sod.
       Still, rain falls like white reeds
Bending in the wind.

Late March, the lengthening days mass on the horizon …
Cancer may be eating my body.

These days, I listen to the sky, blue hooks and foliage,
       Celestial radio riff.
Endless addition and subtraction, and always
The same result – terminus, zero.

Sixty-thousand men once built a lake of mercury
To catch the rising sun –
To be slaughtered by the Emperor
       Who decorated each decapitated corpse
With red bracts of Bougainvillea blossom.

If time stops at any given point, (all of which must exist
       Simultaneously, unless only one persists) …
Along this line, ideas form at the speed of light,

Holy theory of everything, with an energy
Less than nothing, giving all the time you want ... no matter ...
       Pink clouds scud across a heedless sky
And the willow buds unfurl like chrysalides.

In another country, men scratch in the earth.

THE GARDENS OF POMPEII

In the gardens of Pompeii, where fields of asphodel
   once dropped white petals and the grass grinds

beneath your feet, where glass trees clink in the wind
   and winter never comes, the streets where children

ran with barking dogs are empty – the clacking
   cobblestones wrapped in centuries of ash –

like black olives petrified in withered vine-leaves.

POETRY FINAL

[1]

Describe the sound when a penny drops
into a wishing-well. Consider the relevance
of the following factors: acoustics, knowledge
of wells, odds of fulfillment, presence of stars.
To be written from the coin's point of view.

[2]

Imagine gravity traded as a commodity.
From a bird's perspective, make a case
for public ownership, apportioned by weight.
Set on an uninhabited island.

[3]

Explain the attraction of the moon.
In no more than thirty-two lines, suggest
a new name for the number *zero*.
Combine the responses in a 12-line pantoum.

[4]

Establish a seamless association between
the following: an executioner's birthday party,
fractal geometry, attention deficit disorder.
Result must be tacitly non-judgmental,
and be suitable for a sixth-grade audience.

[5]

Bonus question – substantiate your findings.

Alex Grant's chapbook *Chains & Mirrors* (NCWN/Harperprints) won the 2006 Randall Jarrell Poetry Prize and the 2007 Oscar Arnold Young Award (Best North Carolina poetry collection). His second chapbook, *The White Book*, was released in 2008 by Main St. Rag Publishing. His poems have appeared in a number of national journals, including *The Missouri Review, Smartish Pace, Best New Poets* 2007, *Arts & Letters, The Connecticut Review, Nimrod* and *Seattle Review*. A recipient of WMSU's Pavel Srut Poetry Fellowship and the Kakalak Anthology of Carolina Poets Prize, he lives in Chapel Hill, NC, with his wife, Tristi, his dangling participles and his Celtic fondness for excess. He can be found on the web at www.redroom.com/author/alex-grant.

LaVergne, TN USA
07 October 2009
160147LV00003B/218/P